At the Top of Their Game

Danica Patrick

Breaking Speed Barriers

Kate Shoup

Cavendish Square

New York

Published in 2018 by Cavendish Square Publishing, LLC
243 5th Avenue, Suite 136, New York, NY 10016

Copyright © 2018 by Cavendish Square Publishing, LLC

First Edition

Library of Congress Cataloging-in-Publication Data

Names: Shoup, Kate.
Title: Danica Patrick : breaking speed barriers / Kate Shoup.
Description: New York : Cavendish Square, 2018. | Series: At the top of their game | Includes index.
Identifiers: ISBN 9781502628336 (library bound) | ISBN 9781502628404 (ebook)
Subjects: LCSH: Patrick, Danica, 1982---Juvenile literature. | Automobile racing drivers--United States--Biography--Juvenile literature. | Women automobile racing drivers--United States--Biography--Juvenile literature.
Classification: LCC GV1032.P38 S47 2018 | DDC 796.72092--dc23

Editorial Director: David McNamara
Editor: Fletcher Doyle
Copy Editor: Rebecca Rohan
Associate Art Director: Amy Greenan
Designer: Jessica Nevins
Production Coordinator: Karol Szymczuk
Photo Research: J8 Media

Printed in the United States of America

**At the Top of Their Game**

Contents

The First Lady

In 2005, during the eighty-ninth running of the Indianapolis 500, a star was born. That star was none other than rookie race car driver Danica Patrick.

"For more than three hours on Sunday—from the time Indianapolis Motor Speedway chairman of the board Mari Hulman George intoned, 'Lady and gentlemen, start your engines,' to the moment British driver Dan Wheldon crossed the finish line under checkered and yellow caution flags—the 23-year-old Patrick gave the boys all they could handle until she had to back off for lack of fuel," noted *Sports Illustrated* of Patrick's spectacular Indy 500 run. "She also gave the sea of 300,000 spectators what they were hoping to witness: history."

That was hardly the first time Patrick had made history. She'd done it as a youngster, winning multiple national go-karting championships. She'd done it as a teen living in England, finishing second at the famous Formula Ford Festival. She'd done it in the month leading up to Indy, first when she qualified fourth, better

Opposite: Danica Patrick wowed spectators during her rookie run at the 2005 Indianapolis 500.

In 2008, Patrick became the first woman ever to win an IndyCar race with her victory in Japan.

Danica Patrick: Breaking Speed Barriers

than any woman before her; and later, when she turned a lap at a blistering 229.880 miles per hour (369.956 kilometers per hour). This was not only the fastest lap ever by a woman at the historic **oval**; it was the fastest set all month by *anyone*—male or female.

Nor would it be the last. In the coming years, Patrick would become the first woman to win an IndyCar race (in 2008); the first woman to **podium** at Indy (in 2009); the first woman to win the pole at the Daytona 500 (in 2013); and countless other firsts.

Patrick's success in a sport dominated by men came as a surprise to everyone—except perhaps Patrick herself. "I'm going to go out there and prove to you time and again that I belong here, that I will race up front, and that I'm a great driver, not just driving for a great team," she told journalists in the days before her famous rookie run at Indy. Patrick's secret? Disregarding her female status. "I've always believed and wanted and trained to be the best at what I'm doing, to be the best *driver*, not the best girl."

Patrick has achieved a great deal. But perhaps her most important achievement is proving that, as written in *USA Today*, "a woman with the right talent can succeed in a male-dominated sport such as auto-racing when she's given the right backing from people who take her seriously." This knowledge has inspired a generation of girls—not just aspiring professional race car drivers, but girls who seek to follow their dreams, whatever they may be. Patrick, who hails from Roscoe, Illinois, put it this way: "I'm a small-town girl who had a dream and a family who helped her believe anything is possible." She continued, "I am living proof that if you work hard and aim high, you can do whatever you set your mind to, even if that makes you different."

Chapter 1

Karting Standout

On March 25, 1982, Beverly Ann Patrick and her husband, Terry Jose Patrick Jr.—T.J. for short—welcomed their first child. They called her Danica Sue. Two years later, a second daughter, Brooke, arrived.

Danica was born in Beloit, Wisconsin. However, she and Brooke grew up just over the Wisconsin–Illinois border in nearby Roscoe, Illinois. In Roscoe, Beverly and T.J. built their own business, manufacturing plate glass. At first, they ran the business from their garage. Soon, it grew into a larger enterprise, complete with a warehouse, an office, and employees. The couple also opened a coffee shop, called Java Hut. Beverly and T.J.'s success was remarkable. Neither had completed college. It was all due to their hard work. "My parents were middle-class working folks," says their oldest daughter.

These days, Roscoe—situated 90 miles (145 kilometers) northwest of Chicago—is a quickly growing suburb of neighboring Rockville, Illinois. But when Danica was young, it was a sleepy,

Opposite: A young Danica Patrick grabbed attention at the annual Toyota Pro/Celebrity Race at Long Beach in 2002.

small town. Only a few thousand people lived there. "It was a lot of country roads," Patrick recalls. She remembers Roscoe fondly. "I am very glad I grew up in a small Midwestern town," Patrick has said. "Roscoe was just a great place to be a kid." It was, she says, "a lot of two-kids-and-a-dog kind of living."

Patrick Starts Karting

When Danica was ten years old, her parents wanted to find some activity the family could do together. They considered buying a pontoon boat. However, Danica's little sister Brooke had a different idea: **go-karts**. One of Brooke's friends had a go-kart, and Brooke thought it looked like fun.

A go-kart is a small, simple racing vehicle. It consists of a lightweight **chassis**, a single seat, and four small wheels, but no **suspension** or **differential**. For power, most go-karts use a small motor, similar to a lawn mower engine. A go-kart produces anywhere from 5 to 20 **horsepower**. Some racing go-karts can reach speeds of up to 80 miles per hour (129 kmh), and can go from 0 to 60 miles per hour (97 kmh) in about three seconds.

It didn't take much to convince T.J. and Beverly to buy two go-karts—one for Brooke and one for Danica. T.J. had been a racer himself. He had raced snowmobiles, motocross, and midget cars. In fact, he and Beverly had met at a snowmobile race. T.J. was competing, and Beverly was working as a mechanic on a friend's machine. Danica says, "I come from a family of adventure-seekers."

In the parking lot of the family glass business, T.J. laid out a go-kart track, using empty paint cans to mark each turn. The girls learned to drive their karts by steering around the cans. Surprisingly, Brooke was faster—at least at first.

Go-karts are small, simple, racing vehicles.

On her first day driving her go-kart, Danica crashed badly. "A brake pin came out, so she didn't have brakes," Brooke recalls. "She went straight into a concrete wall"—at about 25 miles per hour (40 kmh). Certain she'd been badly injured, T.J. sprinted to his daughter's side. Fortunately, although the kart was ruined, Danica was unhurt. She was also undeterred. All she cared about was when her go-kart would be fixed.

"The exhilaration I felt when I stepped on the pedal of my first go-kart was enough to hook me for life," Danica says. "I loved going fast and steering my kart around tight corners and barreling down the straightaways. I felt a freedom unlike anything I had experienced before."

A Racer Is Born

Soon after receiving their go-karts, the Patrick sisters began competing at a nearby go-kart track called Sugar River Raceway, located in Brodhead, Wisconsin. "We grew up watching racing and with my parents racing," Brooke recalls. "So the thought of us to do it wasn't some stretch."

Danica loved racing. Brooke, however, quickly gave it up. "I had one day where I got in like four different accidents," Brooke recalls. That was enough for her.

In the beginning, Danica was not terribly successful on track. During her first race, the winners quickly lapped her. But "six months into my first season, I was setting track records at the local karting track," she said. Patrick finished that first season second in the points championship. There were twenty drivers in all.

By her second season, Patrick was no longer satisfied with dominating races at her local track. "As my karting career progressed,

Danica Patrick wore lime green as part of her fire suit as a young driver as well as after she became a professional.

Famous Karters

Danica Patrick wasn't the only driver to get his or her start in go-karts. Many famous drivers developed their skills by competing in karts. For example, Formula One stars like Max Verstappen, Sebastien Vettel, Nico Rosberg, Lewis Hamilton, Fernando Alonso, Jenson Button, Kimi Räikkönen, Michael Schumacher, Alain Prost, and the late Ayrton Senna drove karts as kids.

Several IndyCar drivers also cut their teeth in karts. One was four-time IndyCar champion Scott Dixon. Another was three-time Indianapolis 500 winner Helio Castroneves. Sebastien Bourdais, who won four consecutive Champ Car championships during the 2000s, drove karts, as did Juan Pablo Montoya, who went on to compete not only in IndyCar but also in Formula One and NASCAR. Speaking of NASCAR, it also features several drivers who got their start in go-karts, including legends like Jeff Gordon and Tony Stewart.

we began to travel longer distances so I could compete in races in various tracks in Michigan, Ohio, Indiana, and Wisconsin," Patrick says. Once again, she says, "I was shattering records everywhere I went." Patrick even set two records in one day at a track in Michigan. At each new circuit, Patrick—clad in a distinctive purple and lime-green fire suit with her name spelled out in bold letters across her chest—made quite the impression. "There was no mistaking who the driver in the purple and lime-green suit was," she recalls.

Over the next several racing seasons, says Danica, "We spent endless hours … in our family car on weekends traveling to and from races." She competed about fifteen weekends per year, with several races per weekend. T.J. served as her crew chief, engineer, coach, manager, and sponsor. Beverly kept statistics. And Brooke was cheerleader-in-chief. Danica recalls, "My family was my team, my crew, my everything." Her parents, she says, "did whatever it took to see to it that I had all of the advantages in racing."

Danica's mother, Beverly, was incredibly supportive. However, it was her father, T.J., who really drove Danica to succeed. "Dad's interest in racing made my entrée possible," says Danica. T.J.'s formula for success was simple: "live, eat, sleep, drink, and breathe racing."

Many parents push their kids to perform, especially in athletics. All too often, this creates conflict or results in burnout. T.J. wisely took a different approach. "He was really hard on me," says Danica, "but he's not someone who was a pusher. He was a puller. … He'd tell me that I could quit tomorrow, but if I wanted to do it, he was going to help me do it right."

Success and Sacrifice

Almost from the start, Patrick enjoyed tremendous success in go-karting. Between the ages of ten and sixteen, she collected numerous regional titles. She also won the World Karting Association Grand National Championship three separate times, at age twelve (1994), fourteen (1996), and fifteen (1997). In 1996, Patrick won thirty-nine of the forty-nine races in which she competed.

This success didn't come without sacrifice. Other activities—like softball, volleyball, basketball, track, band, and choir—took a back seat as racing became the priority. So, too, did cheerleading. In fact, Patrick was kicked off the Hononegah Community High School cheerleading squad in the tenth grade for missing too many games and practices. Patrick also missed out on proms and homecoming dances, but she didn't mind. None of those things set her apart the way racing did. (Working was also difficult. For a time, Patrick worked at the Java Hut, owned by her parents. After she was forced to skip too many shifts, Beverly had no choice but to fire her!)

"She was a good student," one of her tenth-grade teachers recalls. "But even at that age, she was more focused on her racing career than she probably was on academics." The reason was simple: "At age ten, I had found my life's passion," says Patrick. "From that point forward, I had a one-track mind. Instead of playing soccer after school or taking piano lessons, I dedicated myself to becoming the best race car driver in the world." She explains, "Dreams of becoming a singer, an engineer, or a veterinarian fell to the wayside. Racing was my focus and sole desire." Once Patrick found racing, she had no career plan B.

Girl Driver

Auto racing (including go-karting) is unusual in that it is one of the few sports in which males and females compete on an equal basis. However, that doesn't mean males and females compete in equal numbers. In fact, when Patrick raced go-karts, she rarely competed against other girls.

Sadly, this posed a problem. "It didn't take long for me to understand that being the only girl driver made me different, and my

Women in Racing

Although Patrick was often the only girl at the go-kart track, she wasn't the first female to compete in motorsports. Several brave women preceded her.

French driver Hellé Nice competed in motorsports during the 1920s and 1930s. Unfortunately, her driving career was cut short by a near-fatal accident in 1936. British driver Kay Petre drove in the 24 Hours of Le Mans three times during the 1930s. She also suffered a serious crash that ended her driving career.

During the 1950s, an Italian driver named Maria Teresa de Filippis became the first woman ever to compete in Formula One. Her top-ten finish at the 1958 Belgian Grand Prix remains the highest-ever finish for a woman in that series.

In 1977, an American driver named Janet Guthrie broke the gender barrier at the Indianapolis 500 when she became the first woman ever to compete in that prestigious event—just six years after the facility dismantled rules barring women from the pit and garage areas (let alone in the **cockpit** of a car). Since then, eight more women have competed in this prestigious race.

Sadly, not everyone embraced these female pioneers in motorsport. "The newspapers were full of drivers saying I was going to kill them on track," recalls Guthrie. According to Humpy Wheeler, former president of Charlotte Motor Speedway, "People said [Guthrie] would give out physically at high speed, that she couldn't make it 500 miles, that she couldn't race at certain times of the month." Fortunately, Guthrie and other female racers proved them wrong.

presence on the track would not always be welcomed," Patrick says. "Almost immediately, the boys were intimidated by my success."

T.J. agrees. "Wherever there was a big race, from Florida to California, Wisconsin to Long Island … there was always the issue with this girl showing up," he explains. "Everybody has the hot dog at their track, and there were times we would go out and damned near lap them." Sometimes, the other drivers or their parents accused Danica of cheating. Other times, boys would try to wreck her because they knew she was going to win. When this happened, T.J. inevitably found himself at odds with the other parents. "We had skirmishes," he says. There was "yelling and screaming."

Patrick didn't let it bother her. As far as she was concerned, she was a *driver*, not a *girl driver*. And she was a competitor, too. It was her nature. "I play hard," she says. "I always have, and I always will. My competitive spirit never allowed me to lay back and let anyone win. It still doesn't. I hope it never will." After all, she says, "What was the point of participating if I wasn't going to try to be the best?" Besides, "My car has no idea if I am male or female."

Patrick also had a lot of confidence. "There's a rare type of certainty that's hard to describe unless you possess it yourself," she says. "It's a level of self-confidence that straddles the line between secure and arrogant. It's a type of knowing—a self-belief that is unaffected by what others think or believe." Patrick had that certainty … that *knowing*.

And she loved what she was doing. "I was a gawky kid who wore thick-rimmed glasses. I had long hair that itched my head under the weight of my helmet, not to mention the worst helmet head you ever saw. But I didn't care."

Next Steps

"Becoming a professional race car driver is what I've worked for since the first day I sat behind the wheel of a go-kart," Patrick says. "From day one, I knew this was my calling, my destiny, my dream—and I knew that someday I would make my dream come true."

However, turning pro in auto racing isn't like turning pro in other sports, like basketball or baseball. With these more traditional sports, the way is clear. You play as a youngster. You make your high school team. Perhaps you play in college. And if you're good enough, you land a pro contract. Not so for drivers. "In auto racing," says journalist Amy Rosewater, "there is no clear-cut path to the top."

This lack of a clear path is just one difficulty drivers face. Another is that auto racing is expensive—far more than most other sports. For example, to play basketball, an athlete need purchase only a basketball and a good pair of sneakers. Similarly, baseball players require only a baseball, bat, mitt, helmet, and cleats. In contrast, a race car driver needs a go-kart or some other car. Add to that the necessary safety equipment such as a helmet and fireproof suit, shoes, and gloves, and the costs rise considerably. There's also the cost of travel to and from tracks as well as entry fees for races. When you add all that together, the costs associated with go-karting can reach thousands of dollars a year. For other types of auto racing, such as NASCAR, IndyCar, and Formula One, the costs run in the millions of dollars.

During Patrick's go-karting years, her parents were able to pay her way. But if Patrick wanted to move to the next level in motorsports, she'd need even more funds—more than her parents

Lyn St. James

Lyn St. James, only the second woman ever to compete in the Indianapolis 500, saw young Danica Patrick's potential immediately.

yn St. James was born in Willoughby, Ohio. In 1973, at the age of twenty-six, St. James, who worked as a secretary and piano teacher, attended a race car driving course with her husband. She was hooked. St. James began participating in **sports car** races.

Like most race car drivers, St. James dreamed of competing in the Indianapolis 500. In 1992, at the age of forty-five, she finally had her chance. After years of working to secure a sponsor, St. James landed a sponsorship deal with J.C. Penney, which she used to obtain a ride with Dick Simon Racing.

On May 2, 1992, St. James passed the mandatory rookie test. (During this test, drivers slowly bring their car up to race speed.) Two weeks later, she successfully qualified for the race with a four-lap average speed of 220.150 miles per hour (354.297 kmh), making her only the second woman to make the field. St. James started the race in the twenty-seventh position but fought her way up to finish eleventh. Thanks to this strong finish, St. James won Rookie of the Year honors—the first woman (and oldest driver) ever to do so. "To get to Indy—and win Rookie of the Year—was so satisfying," says St. James, who went on to compete in six more Indianapolis 500 races before retiring from racing in 2001.

These days, St. James focuses her efforts developing female drivers through her foundation. "I've had an impact on these other gals," says St. James. "It makes me incredibly proud."

could provide. ("We spent everything we had," T.J. once told a reporter.) That meant she'd need a sponsor. There are different types of sponsors. Some sponsors are wealthy individuals who have a personal interest in racing. More commonly, sponsors are companies that partner with drivers and teams to advertise their products or services. Usually, that means placing a decal of the company's logo on the car and patches on the driver's and crew members' suits. Without sponsors, Patrick says, drivers like her would be "driving a cab."

She had no idea how to find a sponsor. Fortunately, she met someone who could help: retired race car driver Lyn St. James. In December 1993, St. James launched an organization called the Women in the Winner's Circle Foundation. Its mission was the advancement of women in the automotive and motorsports industries, especially women who dreamed of becoming professional race car drivers. To that end, the foundation organized a driver-development program for young female drivers. In addition to helping these future stars hone their racing skills, the program exposed them to the business side of the sport—including how to approach sponsors.

When Patrick was fourteen years old, she attended the Women in the Winner's Circle driver-development program. St. James immediately saw her potential. "[Danica] had an intensity that is unusual for someone that age," St. James says. Of all the young drivers St. James had coached, Patrick was among the best. "I saw Danica as extraordinary," she says. St. James took a special interest in helping Patrick achieve her dreams.

In 1997, St. James invited Patrick and her family to attend the Indianapolis 500. She introduced Patrick to several famous drivers, team owners, and officials—excellent contacts for an aspiring driver. One of these was a Texas oil man named John Mecom Jr.., who had once owned an IndyCar team and was passionate about racing. He took an interest in Patrick's career. He knew she was talented, and he liked her determination. He believed she had what it took to succeed. Two years later, Mecom Jr.'s son, John Mecom III—also a Texas oilman—offered to sponsor Patrick. With his support, and that of her family, sixteen-year-old Danica Patrick was ready for her next step as a driver.

Chapter 2

Next Steps

Danica Patrick found herself at a crossroads. "I knew that if I was going to fulfill my dream of becoming a professional race car driver, my life would have to take a drastic turn," she says. Simply put, Patrick was no longer satisfied competing in go-kart races. She was ready to try her hand at a new type of racing: **open-wheel**. An open-wheel race car is one that has wheels that stick out from the body of the car. Some open-wheel cars feature wings or other **aerodynamic** features. Like a go-kart, an open-wheel car seats only one person.

The absolute best place to learn how to drive an open-wheel race car is England. As Patrick's mother Beverly says, "If you want to be the best lawyer, you go to Harvard. If you want to be the best driver, you go to England." And so, in 1998, sixteen-year-old Patrick quit school (she would later earn her GED, which is equivalent to a high-school diploma), packed her bags, and moved far from her friends and family to Milton Keynes, England, where she would remain for three years. Backed by her parents and John Mecom III,

Opposite: Patrick wowed fans and drivers alike at the 2000 Formula Ford Festival at Brands Hatch, England, where she placed second.

Motorsports Series

There are many different series in motorsports. One series is Formula One. Another is IndyCar. NASCAR is also a series, as is IMSA.

Each series uses its own type of vehicle. For example, both Formula One and IndyCar use open-wheel cars, although the specifications of these cars are quite different. In contrast, NASCAR features **stock cars**, which have the same basic frame and shape as a typical family sedan. And IMSA runs high-end **sports cars**, such as Audis, Corvettes, and Porsches. IMSA also features **sports prototypes**. Sports prototypes are often designed by automotive manufacturers to incorporate top-of-the-line technology. In addition, each series has its own rules and sets its own schedule.

Some series, like the ones mentioned here, are quite famous. Others are less so. These less-popular series are often development series that serve as important testing grounds for up-and-coming drivers. Formula Vauxhall was one such development series.

who also agreed to become her manager, Patrick would compete in a motorsports series called Formula Vauxhall. Formula Vauxhalls then were open-wheel cars that featured a 150-horsepower engine and were capable of reaching speeds of 150 miles per hour (241 kmh).

Competing in a series like Formula Vauxhall was "the best

possible preparation for open-wheel racing," says Patrick. "I had no idea what I was getting myself into, but I had to listen to my gut and just go for it."

A Hostile Environment

"When you race in England as a young person … it's a very hostile environment," says Patrick. She describes development series like Formula Vauxhall as "a ruthless prep league for drivers from all over the world." Former IndyCar driver and current team owner Bob Rahal agrees. He describes the development series in England as "automotive gang warfare" and the "motor racing equivalent of a street fight."

Driving in a development series in England is difficult for any driver. But for Patrick, it was perhaps even worse. According to Patrick's father T.J., this was for two reasons: "They don't like Americans, let alone women."

"Upon my arrival, I placed unconditional trust in the team, the mechanics, the engineer, and my managers who sponsored my trip abroad," Patrick recalls. "I fully believed they had my best interests at heart." Unfortunately, this optimism would quickly prove unfounded. Her British engineers and mechanics turned their backs on her, focusing instead on her European counterparts. As a result, Patrick "never received the kind of attention, equipment, or guidance [she] expected" and "had no chance of competing on an equal level with the other drivers." This shook her confidence in her driving.

For Patrick, the anti-American sentiment was painful enough. The sexism was even worse. Indeed, she quickly discovered that the racing community in England was even more sexist than the one in

The Brands Hatch motor-racing circuit hosted its first big race in 1960.

the United States. As the only girl in the series, says Patrick, "I knew I'd be dealing with the gender issue ... but I had no concept of how extreme the bias and chauvinistic attitude would become nor the emotional impact it would have on me." She explains, "the people I came into contact with were very old-fashioned in their thinking, especially in their sexist view of women and their role in society."

One day, Patrick had enjoyed a particularly good day on the track, besting all her male rivals by more than a second during practice. Rather than congratulating Patrick, her team owner berated the boys on her team. "You're being beat by a *girl*," he spat out. Needless to say, this frustrated Patrick. "Being a girl described me, but it never defined me, at least not in my eyes," she says. "I wish I could say that was true in everyone else's eyes." There was no doubt about it, says Patrick: "Racing in England was definitely a good ol' boys club."

Ultimately, she realized that success was the best revenge. She knew that as a woman and an American, there was nothing she could say to these men to command their respect. She would just have to prove herself by "going the fastest or winning races."

Handling Loneliness

"England was tough on every level," Patrick recalls of her time abroad. "My overall experience during my three-year stay in England was lonely, depressing, and isolating."

Alone in England, thousands of miles from her family, Patrick tried to make friends. "I was desperate to fit in with the guys," she says of her fellow drivers. "I tried to make friends with the other drivers, but the truth is they didn't want to be friends." She explains, "We weren't in England to be buddies. We were there to be competitors."

Their rejection hardened Patrick. "I turned inward," she says. "I became unapproachable, cold, thick-skinned." Soon, her parents grew concerned. "Whenever I came home for a visit, my parents commented on how different I was. … My mom kept telling me … that I had grown colder. … My parents tell me I've never been the same since England."

Poor Choices

Like many young people who struggle, Patrick made some poor choices in England. One was drinking alcohol. "All of the kids racing at Milton Keynes were living away from home, with no supervision, no real role models, and a lot of temptation," Patrick recalls. "We all drank more than we should have." She knew this was a mistake, but "at sixteen years old, it was the only way I could feel that I belonged."

Patrick also made the mistake of becoming romantically involved with a few of her fellow drivers. These relationships inevitably ended up in heartbreak. Patrick began to doubt herself not just on the track, but off it, too. "I began to wonder, what was wrong with me?"

Her actions didn't just put her confidence at risk. It put her job on the line. "Word had gotten back to my managers that I was misbehaving." Having learned that Patrick was staying out too late and taking poor care of her body (her excessive drinking had caused her to gain weight), "My managers were furious. They had a lot of money tied up in my racing, and they wanted to protect their investment as well as their good name. They were considering cutting me loose."

This scared Patrick straight. She called her managers and told them she would change. "I wanted to get my life back on track and was willing to do whatever they wanted to not lose my ride." Fortunately, they gave her another chance. After that, "My motivation was to show my parents and managers that I was serious about redirecting my life." That meant no more drinking or partying.

Life in England Improves

In 1999, things in England improved. Patrick finished ninth overall in the competitive British Formula Vauxhall Championship. But it was the next year that things *really* turned around. That year, backed in part by Ford Motor Company, Patrick switched teams to compete in the competitive British Zetec Formula Ford series, one of the most important series outside Formula One.

The highlight of Patrick's 2000 season occurred during the Formula Ford Festival. At this famous event—held at Brands Hatch, a famous British **road course**—more than one hundred developmental drivers from all over Europe compete. For this race, Patrick's team supplied her with a different car—one that had until then been driven by a teammate. She discovered that despite being secondhand, this car "was better than any car I had driven during my first couple of years abroad." Armed with proper equipment, Patrick found herself running toward the front all weekend.

Patrick qualified ninth for the feature race—ninth, out of more than one hundred drivers! Before long, she had charged into sixth position. Then, an accident occurred. Rather than prompting a **caution period**, as most accidents do, this one was sufficiently messy to stop the race entirely until it could be cleaned up. (During a caution period, cars remain on track, but travel at a much lower speed for safety reasons.)

During the break, Patrick gave herself a pep talk. "I could do better," she says. "I knew I could. Since when was I ever satisfied with sixth place?" When the race resumed, says Patrick, "I never looked in my rearview mirror again. I looked forward, passing car after car until I found myself racing in third position."

With two laps to go, the two leaders collided, and one spun out. Suddenly, Patrick was in second place—a position she would hold for the rest of the race. It was the highest finish ever for an American at that event.

Returning Stateside

Although her time in England was incredibly difficult, Patrick says "It was a necessary period of time for teenage self-exploration and efforts toward finding—if not deepening—my inner strength. My experiences in England taught me how to deal with difficult people, characteristics, and circumstances. I learned whom I could trust and whom not to trust."

Patrick concludes, "In the end, one of my greatest lessons was learning you need to clear the path you walk on yourself because no one else is really interested in clearing it for you."

Eventually, it was time for Patrick to move back home. In 2001, she left Great Britain for good. Back in the United States, she contemplated her next move. She decided to seek a ride in the Formula Atlantic series. It was "the obvious progression for me professionally," Patrick says. Like Formula Ford, Formula Atlantic was a development series for up-and-coming open-wheel drivers. It featured races all across the United States, Canada, and Mexico. However, things didn't happen for her right away. "I went several months without driving, something I hadn't done since I was ten years old and something I didn't expect." This was hard on her.

Finally, Patrick was given the opportunity to conduct several driving tests for Bob Rahal, who owned a race team. Rahal, himself a former IndyCar driver, had been tracking Patrick's career for some time. "He's a behind-the-scenes looker," says Patrick of Rahal. In 2002, after winning an event in Long Beach, she joined Rahal's team. However, she would not run Formula Atlantic immediately. Instead, she would complete a partial season of the Barber Dodge Pro Series, yet another developmental program. She competed in half the races that season with impressive results, including two top-ten finishes as well as a top-five. "I know Bob Rahal was taking a chance in offering me a ride," Patrick says. She didn't want to let him down.

In 2003, Rahal decided Patrick was ready for Formula Atlantic and signed her for a full season. She was the first woman ever to race that series full time. Patrick didn't fail to impress. She scored five top-ten finishes and three top-fives. She also earned two podiums: a third-place finish in Monterrey, Mexico, and a second-place finish in Miami. Patrick was the first woman ever to podium [finish in the top three] in Formula Atlantic. She finished the season sixth overall.

The next season proved even more successful. Patrick earned the **pole position** in Portland, Oregon—once again the first woman to do so. She also enjoyed even better results: two top-ten finishes, seven top-fives, and three podiums, including a second-place finish in Portland. Such strong results earned Patrick a third-place finish overall.

To her disappointment, Patrick didn't win a race in the Formula Atlantic series. Still, Rahal believed she'd proven her worth. "Her talent was obvious," he says. But it was Patrick's commitment that really impressed him. "There are a lot of talented people in the world who don't have the mental discipline or determination that Danica has." Rahal adds, "That perseverance is what makes the heart of a champion."

Moving Up to IndyCar

In December 2004, Rahal announced that he had signed Patrick for a full-time ride in the IndyCar series. IndyCars are open-wheel race cars that are designed to minimize **drag**, or air resistance. They are extremely fast, reaching speeds of up to 240 miles per hour

Bob Rahal

Bob Rahal was born in 1953 in Medina, Ohio. His father, Mike, was a Lebanese immigrant. Mike owned a successful food wholesale and distribution business. But it was Mike's weekend hobby that really piqued young Bobby's interest: racing sports cars. Bobby dreamed of doing the same.

"In the Rahal family," writes journalist Thomas O'Keefe, "race car driving was done primarily for fun and it was not regarded as a serious line of work." But Rahal eventually realized that one *could* indeed make a living as a race car driver—and he intended to do so.

During the early 1970s, Rahal worked his way up the sports-car ranks, winning an important championship in 1974. The next year, he landed atop the rankings in Formula Atlantic. Rahal then moved to Europe, where he competed in the Formula Two series, which is just one step below Formula One.

In 1978, Rahal seized the opportunity of a lifetime: competing in a Formula One race. "I don't even think they expected me to qualify," recalls Rahal, "but the car was pretty good." Rahal did qualify but was forced to retire from the race due to mechanical problems. This marked both the beginning and the end of Rahal's Formula One career.

Four years later, Rahal signed with an IndyCar team, the start of a seventeen-year run in that series. During this period, Rahal won twenty-four races—including the 1986 Indianapolis 500—and three championships.

Today, Rahal owns an IndyCar team as well as a sports car team. He also owns more than a dozen car dealerships.

Bob Rahal gave Danica Patrick her break in American open-wheel racing.

Patrick immediately made waves in the IndyCar series.

(386 kmh). Patrick's training in the various development series prepared her well to handle these high-speed machines.

"Signing Danica was an easy decision for me," Rahal has said. "Danica is the real deal." For her part, Patrick was thrilled. "I know Bob Rahal was taking a chance on offering me a ride," she said at the time. "He didn't have to take me on … I believe he really wants what's best for me." In England, Patrick had been left to founder on her own. Finally, she'd found a team that provided the support she both needed and deserved.

Keeping Fit …

Even though drivers are sitting when they compete, auto racing is physically taxing. The drivers' upper bodies must be extremely strong. That's because when they drive, they fight a strong gravitational pull while turning the vehicle. This gravitational pull, sometimes called **G-force**, is twice what a fighter pilot feels while maneuvering a jet. It is very difficult to steer while under this level of pressure. For this reason, many drivers—including Patrick—do extensive weight training.

Drivers don't just need strength, however. They also need endurance. Some races last as long as four hours, and drivers need to stay sharp from start to finish. To prepare for this, many drivers train by performing intense cardiovascular exercises, such as running or cycling. Although Patrick used to run between forty and sixty minutes every single day to stay fit, now she prefers interval training.

Patrick also practices yoga a few times a week. She does this mostly for stretching. However, there are other upsides, too. "It's relaxing," she says. "It's calming to me." She also benefits from yoga's focus on breathing. "When things get tense, it's in through the nose and out through the mouth. It's longer breaths, and that inevitably calms your heart rate and calms you down."

... And Falling in Love

In 2001, Patrick suffered an injury while practicing yoga. Bob Rahal suggested she visit a physical therapist he knew named Paul Hospenthal.

"We got along from the first moment he walked into the room," Patrick recalls of Hospenthal. A native of Tacoma, Washington, who had competed in track and field at the college level, Hospenthal was smart, confident, and cool. He was also, Patrick would quickly discover, extremely good at his job.

To thank Hospenthal for treating her injury, Patrick invited him to dinner. He accepted. "We went for sushi and talked for hours,"

Danica Patrick and Paul Hospenthal were married after overcoming quite a few obstacles.

Danica Patrick: Breaking Speed Barriers

says Patrick. Two days later, she underwent a second treatment. This time, Hospenthal asked her out. Soon, their romance bloomed.

There were just three problems. One, Patrick lived in Columbus, Ohio, while Hospenthal resided in Phoenix, Arizona. This posed a snag. "Maintaining a long-distance relationship with Paul took a lot of will and want," she says. Nevertheless, they managed it. Two, Hospenthal was seventeen years Patrick's senior. This initially gave T.J. pause (he eventually came around) but Patrick didn't mind. Three, Hospenthal was a Catholic, while Patrick was "raised in a home with no real religious beliefs." If she wanted to get married in a church in a wedding Mass celebrated by a priest, which she wanted, she had to become Catholic. No matter. Patrick agreed to convert.

In 2004, Hospenthal proposed to Patrick. She excitedly accepted. On November 19, 2005, surrounded by their friends and family, the two exchanged wedding vows.

Chapter 3

IndyCar Sensation

When Patrick joined IndyCar in 2005, the series was ready for her. Once incredibly popular, IndyCar had suffered a terrible decline since the mid-1990s. Patrick, series officials believed, could prove useful in attracting new fans. She was a young, talented, and beautiful woman—just what the series needed.

To understand the reason behind the series' decline, it helps to grasp its long and storied history. The IndyCar series has its roots in the Indianapolis 500. This race is more than one hundred years old and remains IndyCar's marquee event. At first, the American Automobile Association governed the IndyCar series. In 1956, Tony Hulman, who in 1945 had purchased the Indianapolis Motor Speedway (IMS), home of the world-famous Indianapolis 500, formed a new governing body for the series: the United States Auto Club (USAC).

In 1978, several team owners grew frustrated with the USAC. They believed it was doing a poor job of governing the sport.

Opposite: Danica Patrick waits for the start of practice for the 2005 Indianapolis 500.

IMS and the Indy 500

The Indianapolis Motor Speedway (IMS) was built in 1909 by four businessmen: Carl Fisher, James Allison, Frank Wheeler, and Arthur Newby. In its early years, workers used 3.2 million bricks to pave the track (hence its nickname, the Brickyard). Now, the track is paved with asphalt, although bricks remain to mark the start-finish line.

Oddly, the first event ever held at IMS wasn't an auto race. It was a hot-air balloon race, which took place in June 1909. Two months later, several

Ray Harroun en route to victory during the 1911 Indianapolis 500-Mile Sweepstakes in his Marmon Wasp.

motorcycle and automobile races took place. In 1910, IMS put on a series of airplane races featuring none other than Orville and Wilbur Wright.

In 1911, officials at IMS organized a 500-mile (805 km) auto race with a $25,000 purse—a spectacular sum. This race, which they called the International 500-Mile Sweepstakes, was contested on May 30, 1911. Ray Harroun piloted a car called a Marmon Wasp to victory. The Indianapolis 500, as the race later became known, has been contested every year since 1911 except during World War I and World War II.

Today, many call the Indianapolis 500 "The Greatest Spectacle in Racing." The event more than lives up to this name. In this thrilling race, thirty-three daring drivers defy death to reach speeds faster than 230 miles per hour (370 kmh) in search of an elusive victory. It's no wonder that an estimated four hundred thousand fans attended the event's one hundredth running in 2016!

Danica Patrick admitted to *USA Today* that even after moving to NASCAR she still thought about racing again at IMS.

"I think that Indy is special to me," she said."The greater the distance between the last time I drove an Indy car and the next time, I wouldn't like that to be too big."

These team owners formed their own governing body, called Championship Auto Racing Teams (CART). This split the series in two, with two separate championships, although drivers from both series continued to compete at Indianapolis. Two years later, CART and USAC reached a compromise: CART would run the championship, but USAC would maintain control of the Indianapolis 500. This reunification marked the beginning of what many call IndyCar's "golden age." The series became wildly popular. It dominated motorsports in North America, drawing top drivers from all over the world, millions of fans, and loads of sponsorship money.

By the late 1980s, cracks began to show. According to John Bickford, stepfather of an incredibly talented young American driver named Jeff Gordon, "The system was broken." In 1990, Bickford and Gordon approached CART teams in search of a full-season ride. "Everyone's response was, 'How much money can you bring?'" Clearly, money, not talent, now determined which drivers landed a ride. Discouraged, Gordon abandoned his IndyCar hopes for a ride in NASCAR, where he would enjoy a long and successful career.

The loss of a popular young American driver like Jeff Gordon to NASCAR bothered Tony Hulman's grandson, Tony George, who had inherited control of IMS in 1989. George was also concerned that CART—which had added several road courses and **street courses** to the IndyCar schedule—had strayed from its oval-track roots. Finally, George believed that costs for competitors had spiraled out of control, making it impossible for smaller teams to compete. These and other concerns prompted George to launch a new series, the Indy Racing League (IRL), in 1996. He wanted to do away with CART and gain control of American open-wheel racing.

Types of Tracks

IndyCar racing features three types of tracks, or circuits: ovals, road courses, and street courses.

An oval is a dedicated racetrack that is oval in shape. Not all oval tracks are identical, however. Some ovals are short. For example, the oval at Iowa Speedway is only 0.875 miles (1.4 kilometers) around. Others are long, like the one at Indianapolis, which is 2.5 miles (4.023 km) around. In addition, some ovals, called superspeedways, feature high banking, while others are more flat. Finally, not all ovals have the same shape. Some are symmetrical. Others have tighter turns on one end of the track and straights of varying lengths. One so-called oval in the IndyCar series, Pocono Raceway, is even more unusual: it features three rather than four turns. Fans call it the "Tricky Triangle."

Like an oval, a road course is a dedicated racetrack. Unlike an oval, however, a road course comes in many configurations, with several turns. Road courses might also feature different types of terrain, such as hills. A street course is like a road course in that it can come in many configurations, has several turns, and might feature different types of terrain. Street courses are different, however, in that they are not dedicated racecourses. Street courses are temporary tracks on city streets. Each type of track requires a different driving style. This means IndyCar drivers have to be the most versatile drivers in the world.

Unfortunately, this plan proved foolhardy. Rather than folding, CART carried on racing. "The result was devastating on both sides," writes journalist Ryan McGee, "splitting an already leaky pool of sponsors and equipment down the middle." Yes, the IRL retained the Indianapolis 500—a blow to CART. But CART (later renamed Champ Car) retained most of the top teams and drivers—a blow to the IRL. Ultimately, both series lost fans and sponsors.

In 2008, Champ Car shut down and most of its teams and drivers migrated to the IRL, which adopted a new name: IndyCar. However, the damage was done. IndyCar was nowhere near as popular or lucrative as it had been before "the split."

A Slow Start ... and a Big Day

Patrick's IndyCar career started with a bang, but not in a good way. "My first race as an IRL driver at the Toyota Indy 300 Homestead-Miami Speedway, came to a crashing end—literally," Patrick recalls. On lap 159, she suffered a severe concussion after being **collected** in an eight-car pileup. By the next race, which occurred two weekends later at Phoenix International Raceway, she was sufficiently healed. This time, Patrick completed the race but finished a disappointing fifteenth. Two weeks after that, Patrick debuted at St. Petersburg, where again, she registered a relatively lackluster performance, finishing twelfth.

Fortunately for Patrick, her slump was temporary. At her next race, in Motegi, Japan, she made a blistering qualifying attempt to nab the second spot on the grid. She went on to lead thirty-two laps of the race. She eventually fell back to fourth but was pleased with her progress. "I now had the confirmation that I could be a real contender in racing," she says. Perhaps more importantly, "Other people now knew it too."

Making History at Indy

Finishing fourth at Motegi was wonderful, but Patrick had a bigger goal in mind: winning the Indianapolis 500. "When I was a kid, watching the Indy 500 was a Patrick family tradition," she once said. To her, "Racing in the Indy 500 is the equivalent of being nominated for an Oscar, playing in the Super Bowl, or finding yourself on center court, playing the finals at Wimbledon." *Winning* the Indy 500, she continued, "is like taking home the award for Best Actress, wearing the championship ring, or raising the silver cup in victory in front of a cheering crowd." To be racing in the Indy 500 was a big deal. Even better, Patrick had a real chance to win. First, however, she would have to survive the month-long ordeal that is Indy. This is no small thing. Drivers endure three weeks of practice, plus two days of qualifying, before the big race. It's a grueling schedule, but Patrick was ready.

Patrick started the month strong, posting the fastest lap during the first practice session. Later, she would post the fastest lap of the entire month, with an average speed of 229.880 miles per hour (369.956 kmh). This was also the fastest lap completed by a woman ever in the history of the Indianapolis Motor Speedway. Clearly, Patrick was fast enough to capture the pole position.

At Indy, a qualifying run involves four laps. Officials then calculate an average of the four lap speeds. The person with the fastest four-lap speed average wins the pole position. Unfortunately, Patrick experienced a **bobble** during her first lap of qualifying.

(A bobble, sometimes called a wiggle, is when a driver nearly loses control of the car, but doesn't.) Fortunately, she made an impressive save, but her speed for that lap was a disappointing 224.920 miles per hour (361.974 kmh). As Patrick put it, this was "much slower than expected but much faster than ending up in the wall." She went on to set the fastest lap of anyone in qualifying, at 227.860 miles per hour (366.705 khm) per hour. However, this was not enough to offset that slow first lap. Patrick's four-lap qualifying average of 227.004 miles per hour (365.328 kmh) per hour would not earn her the pole. She would start from the fourth position. This was disappointing. However, it was still the highest start ever for a female driver at Indianapolis—"something to be proud of," says Patrick.

Her success during practice and qualifying launched a media frenzy. Suddenly, everyone wanted a piece of this fast, feisty, female driver. Patrick found herself overwhelmed. "My schedule off the track had become more grueling than the time I spent on the track practicing and qualifying for this month-long event." Still, she says, "I wanted to do as much media as I could because I wanted the IRL series to grow and become a household name for fans."

Race Day

At last, race day arrived. Finally, "after an exhausting week of nonstop press and media interviews and appearances, it was time to focus on the task at hand—winning," says Patrick.

For a time, it seemed as if Patrick might do just that. On lap fifty-seven (of two hundred), she claimed the first position, becoming the first woman ever to lead at Indy. She remained there until lap

Opposite: Patrick started the 2005 Indianapolis 500 from fourth position, the highest-ever start for a female driver.

IndyCar Sensation

seventy-nine, when she dropped into third position. Unfortunately, during her next pit stop, Patrick stalled her car as she exited her pit box, losing valuable time and tumbling to sixteenth position.

Over the next one hundred laps, Patrick fought her way back to the top ten. However, she was again shuffled to sixteenth when, on a restart following a caution period, she spun her car, damaging its nose cone and front wing and triggering yet another caution period. This happened on lap 155. Patrick pitted immediately to replace the nose cone and wing. She pitted again on lap 159 to take on more fuel. When the caution period ended, Patrick was in ninth position, the last driver on the **lead lap**—one of just two drivers with a near-full tank of fuel.

At this critical moment, Bob Rahal made a decision: Patrick would not pit again. This was risky. Under normal conditions, drivers could complete only thirty laps running top-speed on a full tank of fuel, but there were forty-one laps to go. Patrick would need to adjust her driving style and speed to conserve fuel. She would also need at least a few laps under caution, during which she could drive even slower. However, if Patrick stayed on track when the leaders made their final pit stop, she could cycle back up to the lead. All she'd have to do then was maintain it. "I didn't think we were fast enough to pass all eight of those guys," Rahal says. So, "we decided to roll the dice."

With thirty laps to go, a driver named Roger Yasukawa's engine blew up on the front stretch. This prompted a much-needed caution period for cleanup. It also prompted the race leaders to dive into the pits for their final stop of the race. Just as Rahal had hoped, Patrick cycled into first position. She remained there for several laps. However, drivers with more fuel and fresher tires eventually

Conserving Fuel

Drivers use a variety of techniques to conserve fuel. One is by **drafting**—that is, driving directly behind another car. This works because the driver in front creates a slipstream. The slipstream results in less drag for the driver in back, enabling them to drive at the same speed as the driver in front without burning as much fuel. (This option was not available to Patrick during the waning laps of the 2005 Indy 500, as she was in the lead.) Another technique drivers use is to smooth out their driving. That is, rather than jamming on the brakes or the accelerator, they smoothly switch from one to the other. Patrick is particularly good at this technique. A third technique is simply to slow down.

caught up. With fourteen laps to go, Dan Wheldon passed Patrick. However, the race wasn't over quite yet. On the same lap, driver Kosuke Matsuura crashed into the wall in turn four, resulting in yet another critical caution period.

As Patrick prepared for the final dash, her engineer transmitted a spoken message to her over the team radio, which she could hear thanks to a speaker in her helmet. "Danica," he said, "we need the restart of the twenty-first century." With ten laps to go, Patrick delivered. She blew by Wheldon as the field thundered into turn one and quickly pulled away to a one-second lead.

It was a lead Patrick could not hold. Wheldon reclaimed the top

On-track Rivalry

Dan Wheldon, a native of Emberton, England, became a full-time IndyCar series driver in 2003. By 2005, he had become one of the series' dominant drivers. That year, in addition to winning the Indy 500, Wheldon won at Homestead-Miami; St. Petersburg; Motegi, Japan; Colorado; and Chicagoland—more than one-third of all the races run that year. He went on to win the overall IndyCar championship by eighty points.

Dan Wheldon celebrating his victory at Indianapolis in 2005, his first of two wins in the event. He also won in 2011.

After outlasting Patrick during the 2005 Indy 500, Wheldon might reasonably have felt snubbed due to the attention she received following the race. And perhaps he did. At the next race, in Texas, fans spotted Wheldon wearing a cheeky T-shirt that read, "Actually Won the Indy 500." Still, Wheldon understood that Patrick's participation in the series raised its profile, which benefited everyone.

Patrick and Wheldon developed a rivalry of sorts. Perhaps the most memorable incident between them occurred at Milwaukee in 2007. The pair made contact on track, causing Patrick to bobble and lose her position. After the race, Patrick confronted Wheldon in pit lane, grabbing his arm and shoving him. However, they made up at the next race.

In 2011, Wheldon won his second Indy 500. Tragically, he was killed later that year in a crash at Las Vegas, leaving behind a wife and two young sons.

Patrick raced at Las Vegas the next year in a NASCAR Nationwide event and made it clear that Wheldon's death still weighed on her mind.

"Time is a healer for sure, but there won't be a time I come here when I don't think of it," she told *Autoweek*. "I think it will never completely escape me, and that's what tragedy will do to you."

position three laps later. That was it for Patrick: she simply did not have enough fuel to run at top speed. Wheldon slowly pulled away and soon claimed victory. Two other drivers, Vitor Meira and Bryan Herta, also passed Patrick in the final laps. Patrick finished fourth—a position she was "pleased with for a rookie but disappointed with as a dreamer, a believer, and as someone who knows she has what it takes to win this race." Still, it was the best finish ever by a female driver. It also earned her Indy 500 Rookie of the Year honors, like her mentor, Lyn St. James, before her, not to mention $380,000 in prize money. "I believed I had a chance to win," says Patrick. "Had another yellow flag come out, I probably would have." Still, she says, "What a ride!" (Later, Patrick would learn that there were still 2.5 gallons (9.5 liters) of fuel in her tank when she crossed the finish line. "I probably should have pushed it a little more," she says. Who knows—she might have won!)

Perhaps more importantly, as noted in *USA Today*, Patrick proved that "a woman with the right talent can succeed in a male-dominated sport such as auto racing when she's given the right backing from people who take her seriously." This stood in sharp contrast to auto-racing pioneer Janet Guthrie's experience. Guthrie writes in her memoirs that one auto executive told her, "No one will give you a winning car because you're a woman." Sadly for Guthrie, this proved to be true.

Patrick's accomplishments quickly made her a star. One week after the race, she made the cover of *Sports Illustrated*—the first IndyCar driver to do so in twenty years. She also appeared on countless TV shows, including *SportsCenter*, *Pardon the Interruption*, *The Today Show*, *Good Morning America*, *The Tony Danza Show*, *Jimmy Kimmel Live*, and *The Late Show with David Letterman*. This

Danica Patrick: Breaking Speed Barriers

Safety Features

Racing is dangerous. Drivers are sometimes injured or even killed on track. Still, IndyCar works hard to keep drivers as safe as possible. All drivers wear a fireproof suit as well as fireproof gloves, shoes, and underclothes. Drivers must also wear a full-faced helmet. This is attached to a head and neck support (HANS) device that rests on the driver's shoulders, which prevents the driver's head from snapping forward in a collision and damaging the neck or skull.

IndyCar also incorporates safety technology into its cars. For example, drivers are strapped tightly into a carbon-fiber tub, which protects them in a collision. Also, certain pieces of the car are attached using tethers to ensure they don't go airborne during a crash. (This is partially in response to an accident in 2015 in which driver Justin Wilson was killed when he was struck in the head by flying debris from another car.)

Tracks, too, have safety features. One is the steel and foam energy reduction (SAFER) barrier, which is used instead of concrete walls. SAFER barriers absorb much of the energy in a crash—energy that would otherwise be absorbed by the car and driver.

When a crash occurs, IndyCar officials immediately dispatch a team of medical professionals and firefighters, called the Holmatro Safety Team, to the scene. This team is noted for its speed, usually reaching the driver in distress within a matter of seconds. Over the years, this team has saved the lives of countless IndyCar drivers.

last appearance was particularly meaningful, as Letterman—
a longtime IndyCar fan—was co-owner of her team, Rahal
Letterman Racing.

More Success

Patrick's success didn't end at Indy. In July, at Kansas Speedway, she
claimed her first IndyCar pole position—the first woman ever to
do so. In August, she claimed her second pole position, at Kentucky
Speedway. And in September, she claimed her third, this time at
Chicagoland Speedway. Patrick's three poles tied the rookie record.
As for race results, Patrick amassed five top-tens and two top-fives
(Motegi and Indy). She finished the season twelfth overall and
earned Rookie of the Year honors. "Coming into the season I said
I wanted to learn and improve," says Patrick. "I also wanted to be
Rookie of the Year at Indy and for the IndyCar series. I set those
goals and accomplished all of them."

Tragedy at the Track

When the first race of her sophomore season, the Toyota 300 at
Homestead-Miami, came around, Patrick was more than ready.
Unfortunately, she and her team would be dealt a terrible blow.
During a pre-race practice, one of Patrick's teammates, a rookie
driver named Paul Dana, collided at an estimated 176 miles per hour
(283.245 kmh) with a stalled car on track. According to one report,
"Dana's car split nearly in half. The chassis flew about 6 feet (1.8 m)
off the ground, and pieces were strewn down the track."

The driver in the stalled car, Ed Carpenter, was miraculously
unhurt. However, Dana died of injuries sustained in the crash.

Paul Dana tragically lost his life at Homestead-Miami.

The Andretti Family

To many, the name "Andretti" is synonymous with open-wheel racing. Three generations of this family have been racers.

The first of these were Mario Andretti and his twin brother Aldo. Aldo suffered two serious crashes, in 1959 and 1969. The second of these ended his driving career. Mario was more fortunate. He enjoyed a long career behind the wheel—one that included a Daytona 500 win (in 1967), an Indy 500 win (in 1969), two CART championships (1969 and 1984), and a Formula One championship (1978). He is one of only two drivers to win a race in NASCAR, IndyCar, and Formula One. (The other is Juan Pablo Montoya.)

Mario's two sons, Jeff and Michael, also became race car drivers. Aldo's son, John, did the same. Unfortunately, a serious accident cut Jeff's career short. John and Michael continued on, however, with Michael winning one CART championship. Michael also spent one season in Formula One.

Michael's son Marco has since joined the fray. In 2006, Marco signed with Andretti Green Racing as a rookie and enjoyed a spectacular year. He very nearly won the Indy 500 (he finished second) and took first place at Sonoma. He has been with the team ever since.

Opposite: Marco Andretti (*center*) with father Michael (*left*) and grandfather Mario (*right*).

Patrick and her remaining teammate, Buddy Rice, were devastated. Concerned about their ability to concentrate behind the wheel, both drivers pulled out of the race. Team owner Bob Rahal was also brokenhearted. He described the event as a "very black day."

Like all drivers, Patrick understands the dangers of racing. But she tries to be philosophical about it. "You're at risk being in your own house," she says. "There's a chance for tragedy every second." This attitude enabled Patrick to refocus following Dana's death. One week later, she competed at St. Petersburg, Florida, where she finished sixth. This was the first of six top-ten finishes she would claim that season, including an eighth at Indy. Patrick also earned two top-fives, at Nashville and Milwaukee. She finished the season ninth overall and was voted Most Popular Driver.

A New Team

At the end of the 2006 season, Patrick was ready for a change. She loved Bob Rahal and appreciated all he had done for her. "I wouldn't be here without him," she told reporters at the time. "I will be forever grateful for what he's done for me." However, the Rahal Letterman Racing team had struggled in 2006, which frustrated Patrick. As she told USA Today, "I just [want] an opportunity with a team that gives me the best chance to win races."

In 2006, she switched to Andretti Green Racing (AGR). "Andretti Green has won more races than anyone else in the series," Patrick said at the time. Indeed, drivers in the AGR stable had won the previous two championships. Not surprisingly, Patrick's decision upset Rahal. "I do believe there is something called loyalty," he told the press. But Patrick felt she had no choice.

AGR welcomed her with open arms. "Danica has shown great talent during her first two seasons in the IndyCar series," team co-owner Michael Andretti said in a team statement. "Our focus has been and always will be on winning races and winning championships. We certainly believe Danica will do that."

Patrick enjoyed a successful 2007 season with AGR. Driving the number-seven car with sponsorship from Motorola, XM Radio, and Go Daddy, she scored eleven top-ten finishes (including an eighth at Indy), four top-fives, and three podiums—the first of her career. These came at Texas, where she finished third; Nashville, another third; and Detroit, where she finished a career-high second. Patrick also led several race laps during the 2007 season. There was no doubt about it: Things were looking up!

A Big Win ... and a New Path

During her first three years in IndyCar, Danica Patrick had shown steady improvement—but she had yet to win a race. By the start of the 2008 season, the pressure to claim her first victory was enormous. On April 20, 2008, all that would change. At the Indy Japan 300 in Motegi, Japan, Patrick became the first woman ever to win an IndyCar race.

She started the race from sixth place, a position she maintained for much of the race. On lap 143 (of 200), a caution period prompted Patrick and most other drivers to pit. Five laps later, just before the restart, Patrick pitted once more—one of just two drivers to do so. (The other was Helio Castroneves.) This savvy strategy, along with Patrick's efforts to conserve fuel, paid off. The race leaders did not have enough fuel to make it to the finish and were forced to pit with five laps to go. Castroneves and Patrick, however, were able to stay on track (in that order). Soon, Patrick passed Castroneves for the lead, which she held to the end. Patrick was overcome with joy. "Finally!" she cried in Victory Lane, fighting back tears.

Opposite: A jubilant Danica Patrick following her 2008 victory at the Indy Japan 300 in Motegi, Japan.

Patrick's parents were thrilled. "It's the best day of my life," T.J. said afterward. "I've dreamed about it, and I'm so proud of her." Bev agreed, noting, "She's worked so hard." Team owner Michael Andretti—the a former IndyCar and Formula One driver and the son of racing legend Mario Andretti—was similarly thrilled. "I'm so happy for her and so proud of her," he told reporters. "It's always been a question of when—not if—she was going to win, and I'm so proud of the way she did it." Even her chief competitor in the race, Castroneves, was complimentary: "She did a great job," he said. "Passed me fair and square."

Patrick's win was particularly moving for her fellow female racers. As Sarah Fisher, the third woman ever to run the Indianapolis 500 and a regular competitor on the IndyCar circuit from 1999 to 2010, put it, "Today marks the celebration for all of us who have chipped away at the barriers that many women have faced in fields that are dominated by men. To finally have a female win an open-wheel race is simply a progression of what Janet Guthrie started."

Continuing in IndyCar

After Motegi, Patrick's next race was in Kansas. She qualified third, but a broken wheel hub cost her the race. This was frustrating, to say the least!

Then came Indy, where things went from bad to worse and worse again. On the day before qualifying, as Patrick drove down pit lane, she accidentally struck a crewmember from a different team. (Fortunately, the man was not seriously hurt.) And although Patrick managed to qualify a respectable fifth, her race was ruined when Ryan Briscoe collided with her on pit lane, putting them both out of the race. Furious, Patrick scrambled out of her car and made for

"Danica Patrick" Rule

In 2008, IndyCar officials mandated that minimum weight requirements for IndyCars include the driver. (Before, the weight requirements applied to the car only.) Patrick believed this was in response to complaints from other drivers who believed she enjoyed an unfair advantage due to her low body weight.

Rival teams estimated that Patrick, who stands at five feet two inches (1.575 meters) tall and weighs just 100 pounds (45.359 kilograms), might enjoy as much as 1 mile per hour (1.6 kmh) of extra speed due to her size. Still, Patrick was frustrated. "In other sports, athletes don't get penalized for being too strong, or too tall, or too fast," she groused to reporters. Besides, as she correctly pointed out, "What I lack in weight I have to more than make up for in body strength." She continued, "Should I complain that men are stronger than I am and therefore they have an unfair advantage driving? I don't think so."

To meet the minimum weight requirements, Patrick was forced to add 35 pounds (15.876 kilograms) of **ballast** to her car. The fact that Patrick won at Motegi after this rule was in place makes her achievement even more impressive.

Briscoe's pit. IMS security intervened, however, preventing Patrick from confronting Briscoe on track in full view of the crowd. For her actions, IndyCar officials fined Patrick $100,000 and placed her on probation. Briscoe received the same punishment.

Patrick went on to earn five top-tens and two top-fives in 2008 and finished the season ranked sixth. In 2009, she did even better, earning five top-tens, four top-fives, and one podium—at Indy. There, Patrick finished third, beating her own record for the highest finish at Indy by a woman. She ended the season ranked fifth overall—a career high, the top driver on her team (now called Andretti Autosport), and the top American driver in the series.

A New Horizon

Before the start of the 2010 IndyCar season, Patrick made a surprising announcement: she would run a limited schedule in the NASCAR Nationwide series. "I'd just like to try it and see how I get on with the cars," she said. "I just think the racing looks like fun." Patrick was hardly the first IndyCar driver to try her hand at NASCAR. Sam Hornish Jr. made the switch in 2006. Dario Franchitti followed in 2008 (although he would return to IndyCar after just one year). Now it was Patrick's turn to try.

Stock cars handle quite differently from open-wheel vehicles. This makes it difficult to switch from one to the other. For this reason, Jimmie Johnson—one of the most successful NASCAR drivers in history, having won seven NASCAR championships (including five in a row between 2006 and 2010)—advised Patrick to take things slow. "If she's serious about doing it, she needs to spend a year or two, while racing IRL, running ARCA, running trucks, running Nationwide and really understanding the difference

NASCAR Series

The National Association of Stock Car Auto Racing (NASCAR) oversees multiple stock-car series all over the world. Internationally, NASCAR governs series in Europe, Mexico, and Canada. In the US, the organization oversees various regional series, the Xfinity Series (formerly the Nationwide Series), and the Monster Energy Series (formerly Sprint Cup). This last series is the highest-level series under the NASCAR banner. Finally, NASCAR controls a truck series. NASCAR is not the only stock car racing organization, however. Another is Automobile Racing Club of America (ARCA). ARCA features a mix of professional and hobby racers.

in the vehicles," Johnson said. "Otherwise, she's going to be put in a tough situation."

Patrick wisely followed Johnson's advice. She continued to run a full IndyCar schedule for Andretti Autosport while she dipped a toe into NASCAR. Because IndyCar took priority, she limited her first season in NASCAR to thirteen Nationwide Series events, driving the number-seven Chevrolet for JR Motorsports under the sponsorship of Go Daddy.

On February 13, 2010, Patrick made her NASCAR Nationwide Series debut, at Daytona. This effort ended early when a twelve-car accident collected Patrick on lap sixty-eight. The next week found

Patrick gets behind the wheel of her car for a practice run for Nationwide Series race at Michigan International Speedway in 2010.

her in Fontana, California, where she finished a disappointing thirty-first. As for her third race—this one in Las Vegas—it ended much like the first one: with Patrick out early thanks to a wreck. Things didn't improve much as the season progressed. Her best finish was a mediocre twenty-first place at Charlotte Motor Speedway.

Patrick's 2010 IndyCar season was a bit less frustrating—though not by much. Perhaps the low point was at Indy. She delivered a poor performance during qualifications, managing only twenty-third position—a career worst. During an interview broadcast over the track loudspeakers, Patrick blamed the failure on her car's setup,

Danica Patrick: Breaking Speed Barriers

The History of NASCAR

During the Prohibition era, which lasted from 1920 until 1933, the production, importation, transportation, and sale of alcohol were outlawed. Still, a thirst for these boozy beverages remained. This prompted the development of a black market for liquor. Much of the alcohol sold on this black market was whiskey made in the Appalachian region. To transport it, **bootleggers** drove small, fast vehicles—many of which were modified for increased speed—which enabled them to outrun the police.

Eventually, the US government repealed Prohibition. However, these fast drivers remained. They had developed a taste for speed, and began racing each other—sometimes for fun, sometimes for money. On March 8, 1936, a collection of these drivers gathered at Daytona Beach, Florida, for a 250-mile (402 km) race. The winner was a driver named Milt Marion. Perhaps more notable was the fifth-place finisher: a young man named Bill France.

In 1947, Bill France formed a series for stock car racers, called the National Championship Stock Car Circuit (NCSCC). Its schedule featured nearly forty races. France enticed drivers to join the series by promising the series champion a check for $1,000 (and a trophy, of course). In 1948, France changed the series' name to the National Association for Stock Car Racing (NASCAR) and solidified its schedule, specifications, and rules.

Since then, NASCAR has grown by leaps and bounds. Today, it is the most popular motorsports series in North America.

describing it as "absolutely awful" and noting that her disappointing qualifying spot was "not my fault." This did not go over with the crowd, which booed loudly. They interpreted her statements as a criticism of her engineers and mechanics. Patrick redeemed herself on race day by charging from twenty-third to finish sixth. There were a few other bright spots in Patrick's 2010 IndyCar season, too. She earned three top-tens, one top-five, and two second-place finishes, and finished the season in tenth place.

Double Duty

Patrick again did double-duty in 2011, competing part-time in the NASCAR Nationwide Series while running a full IndyCar schedule.

On the NASCAR side, Patrick competed in twelve Nationwide Series events. She saw considerable improvement, scoring three top-fifteen finishes, two top-tens, and one top-five. This last result, an impressive fourth place at Las Vegas, was the best ever by a woman in a top-level NASCAR series.

Patrick's IndyCar season went somewhat less smoothly. Once again, she struggled during qualifying at Indianapolis, although this time, she wasn't the only one. All three of her Andretti Autosport teammates—Mike Conway, Marco Andretti, and Ryan Hunter-Reay—found themselves in the same boat. None of the Andretti drivers made the field on the first day of qualifying, and the second day didn't go much better. Patrick was nearly denied an opportunity to even attempt a qualifying run due to rain. However, with just over an hour left in the qualifying session, she finally got her chance. She qualified comfortably in the twenty-sixth position—a career worst, but a relief nonetheless. (She would go on to finish the race a respectable tenth.)

Bursting the Bubble

Patrick made the 2011 Indy field comfortably, but her Andretti Autosport teammates, Mike Conway, Marco Andretti, and Ryan Hunter-Reay, weren't so lucky. Conway made three qualifying runs but failed to make the field. Hunter-Reay and Andretti did make the field, but just barely. Then, a driver named Alex Lloyd bumped Andretti out, putting Hunter-Reay **on the bubble**. Andretti then made yet one more qualifying run, peeling out of pit lane with less than a minute left in the session, and bumped Hunter-Reay out. This was nothing short of a disaster. Hunter-Reay's sponsorship that year depended on his participation in the Indy 500. Failing to make the field put his whole season at risk. Fortunately for him, legendary driver and team owner A. J. Foyt bailed Hunter-Reay out by offering to put him in one of the Foyt cars, which had been qualified by a part-time driver.

A Sad End

As bad as Indy was—particularly qualifying—it was nothing compared to what happened during the final IndyCar race of the season, at Las Vegas. On the eleventh lap of the race, a driver named Wade Cunningham experienced a bobble on the front straight and made light contact with two other drivers, James Hinchcliffe and J.R. Hildebrand. This set off a terrible chain reaction.

Will Power (*center*) goes airborne in the crash at Las Vegas that claimed the life of Dan Wheldon (*in flames at top left*).

Danica Patrick: Breaking Speed Barriers

A Big Win ... and a New Path

Dealing with Criticism

Patrick's lackluster results in NASCAR have brought criticism. In 2013, former driver Kyle Petty called her a "marketing machine." He continued, "She's come a long way, but she's still not a race car driver. And I don't think she's ever going to be a race car driver." Petty's father, the legendary Richard Petty, shares a similar view. When asked in 2014 if Patrick would ever win a Sprint Cup race, Richard Petty responded, "[Only] if everybody else stayed home."

Other drivers have come to Patrick's defense. "I thought he was a little rough on Danica," Dale Earnhardt Jr. says of Richard Petty. Kevin Harvick agrees, noting that newer NASCAR drivers like Patrick aren't given the practice time he and his peers received. "Her test sessions are actually during races, with a lot of media attention. So it's really a lot of unfair scrutiny." And Ricky Stenhouse Jr. notes, "I think she's proved she can drive these race cars." For her part, Patrick responds to such criticism with a simple and honest "I really don't care." She explains, "I work really hard, I'm happy with who I am, happy with what I do."

Cunningham lost control of his car and swerved, causing Hildebrand to drive up over the top of him. Cunningham also collected two other drivers, Jay Howard and Townsend Bell, before colliding with the wall. Vitor Meira swerved to avoid the melee but quickly lost control of his own car, collecting Charlie Kimball, E. J.

Viso, and Tomas Scheckter. Paul Tracy then collided with Scheckter, and Pippa Mann—swerving to avoid another car—went over the top of Tracy. Will Power was launched airborne, landed sideways on the track, and rolled over. Finally, Dan Wheldon ran over the top of Charlie Kimball, tumbled some 325 feet (99 meters) through the air, and tangled with the catch fence cockpit-first before sliding to a stop on the track.

This triggered a caution period for the remaining drivers, of which Patrick was one. "The debris we all had to drive through the lap later, it looked like a war scene from *The Terminator* or something," driver Ryan Briscoe recalls. "There were just pieces of metal and car on fire in the middle of the track with no car attached to it and just debris everywhere." The next lap, officials halted the race to better assess the damage.

Most of the drivers suffered only minor injuries. Some were more serious, however. Hildebrand hurt his sternum. Pippa Mann suffered severe burns on one hand. Will Power broke his back. But even these drivers considered themselves lucky. They had survived. Tragically, Dan Wheldon was not as fortunate. The charismatic two-time Indy 500 winner was airlifted to an area hospital but was declared dead on arrival due to blunt-force trauma to the head.

Out of respect for Wheldon, officials cancelled the race. To pay tribute, eighteen of the surviving drivers—those whose cars were still in one piece—performed a five-lap salute. Patrick was among these. As they drove slowly around the track, bagpipes played "Danny Boy" and "Amazing Grace" over the track loudspeaker.

Patrick was visibly shaken by Wheldon's death. "There are no words for today," she tweeted afterward. "Myself and so many others are devastated." That Patrick had ended the 2011 season with eight top-tens (including Indy) and a single top-five, finishing tenth in the championship, hardly seemed to matter.

Full-Time NASCAR Driver

Las Vegas was Patrick's last IndyCar race. In August of 2011, she announced that she'd be leaving IndyCar to drive NASCAR full-time during the 2012 season. She would run a full Nationwide Series season. She would also do a limited run in the Sprint Cup Series—the top series in NASCAR.

In 2011, Patrick enjoyed some success in the Nationwide Series. She earned fifteen top-fifteens and four top-tens (including a season-high eighth at Texas) and finished tenth in the standings. She also won her first pole in the series, at the season-opener at Daytona—only the second woman in NASCAR history ever to do so in a top NASCAR series—and led laps in six of thirty-three races. And, just as she had been in IndyCar, Patrick was voted most popular driver in the series. Sprint Cup proved a bit more frustrating, however. In that series, Patrick ran ten races and managed only one top-twenty finish—and several crashes. She finished sixty-second in the points.

In 2013, Patrick signed with Stewart-Haas Racing for a full-time Sprint Cup ride. She made an immediate impression, winning the pole at the Daytona 500—the first woman ever to do so. She went on to lead several laps of the race and finished eighth, once again making history. However, the rest of Patrick's season was less impressive. She managed just three top-twenty finishes and finished twenty-seventh in the points, although she did become the first woman ever to complete a full Sprint Cup schedule.

Patrick's next three seasons in NASCAR continued in much the same vein. She finished the 2014 Sprint Cup season in

Quotes Concerning Patrick

"I saw Danica as extraordinary."

—Lyn St. James

"I was willing to gamble on Danica because I knew she was willing to give back more than we gave and also determined and committed to develop her best effort each and every race. She always rises to the occasion."

—Bob Rahal

"When she's in the car, she's a race driver, not a woman."
—Former Rahal Letterman Racing team manager Jimmy Prescott

"Watching your daughter lead the Indy 500 with seven laps to go—there's nothing like it. It's impossible to describe."

—T.J. Patrick

"On a personal level what I appreciated about Danica was her work ethic. She is a real professional. She is flat-out—a complete package in many ways ... I have great respect for her."

—Mario Andretti

"I love having [Danica] in the sport. I think she's great for the sport."

—Jeff Gordon

"Provocative. Combative. Competitive. Danica Patrick packs a lot into her 5-foot-2 frame."
—Journalist Mike Brudenell

"I could be described as extremely confrontational. I prefer to see it as brutally honest."

—Danica Patrick

In Good Company

Patrick is one of only fourteen drivers to lead both the Daytona 500 and the Indianapolis 500, and one of only seven to lead at least five laps in each race. (The other members of this small club include A. J. Foyt, Mario Andretti, Robby Gordon, Juan Pablo Montoya, A.J. Allmendinger, and Tony Stewart.) Patrick's real dream, however, is to win a race in both IndyCar and NASCAR. That would put her in the same company as Dan Gurney, Parnelli Jones, Foyt, Johnny Rutherford, Mario Andretti, John Andretti, Robby Gordon, Stewart, and Montoya. Stewart's feat, winning *series titles* in both IndyCar (1997) and NASCAR (2002, 2005, 2011), remains elusive.

twenty-eighth position. In both 2015 and 2016, she was twenty-fourth. She collected no poles or wins, although she did manage five top-ten finishes during this stretch.

Still, Patrick has high hopes for her future in NASCAR. She has a multi-year deal with Stewart-Haas Racing. She'll be switching from a Chevrolet engine to a Ford. And of course, she'll keep learning. "If we can put all the other factors into place that help the car be fast and build great cars and have great manufacturer support," she says, "then maybe it'll all come together."

Danica Patrick: Breaking Speed Barriers

Patrick poses with her car after qualifying for the 2016 Daytona 500. She started from the number sixteen position in the forty-driver field.

A Big Win ... and a New Path

Chapter 5

Patrick's Legacy

Danica Patrick has been a professional race car driver since she was twenty-one years old. Now in her mid-thirties, she shows no signs of slowing down. "I want to be one of the few drivers that has won an IndyCar race and a NASCAR [race]," she says. "That is the goal every weekend."

Patrick has at least a few more years to make that goal a reality. In August 2015, she signed a multi-year contract extension with Stewart-Haas Racing to continue racing in the NASCAR Sprint Cup Series. "It really does feel like family here," she says of the organization. She also has had no trouble attracting sponsors. When difficulties arose with one sponsor early in 2017, Aspen Dental increased its commitment to Patrick and became her lead sponsor.

"I love working with organizations that care about people, and teaming up with a group that has such an important mission—breaking down barriers and helping patients get the dental care they need—is very rewarding," she said in a team press release.

Opposite: In 2013, Danica Patrick became the first woman ever to win the Daytona 500 pole.

Similar Path

Patrick's team, Stewart–Haas racing, is co-owned by Tony Stewart. Like Patrick, Stewart got his start in in go-karts. Like Patrick, he launched his professional racing career in IndyCar (winning the series title in 1997). And like Patrick, he later switched to NASCAR, where he has enjoyed a nearly two-decade career and claimed three championships.

In 2008, Stewart—a native of Columbus, Indiana, where he still resides—partnered with team owner

Patrick talks with Tony Stewart, co-owner of Stewart–Haas Racing.

Gene Haas to launch Stewart-Haas Racing, making Stewart one of only a handful of NASCAR driver/owners. Many in NASCAR saw this as a "massive, if not impossible, challenge." However, Stewart has made it work. Indeed, in 2011, Stewart became the first owner-driver to win a NASCAR Sprint Cup title in nearly twenty years.

Stewart is also a devoted philanthropist, supporting charitable causes including the chronically ill and physically disabled, animals, and drivers who are injured in motor racing. To date, his foundation has awarded more than $6.5 million to charities throughout the United States (which may go a long way toward explaining why Stewart was named "Most Caring Athlete" by *USA Weekend* in 2004).

What's next for Stewart—who retired from Sprint Cup racing at the end of 2016—is anyone's guess. "I couldn't have asked for more out of this life," he says. "I feel like I'm a very, very fortunate person, so no matter what happens, no matter how long I race or don't race, the goals and everything that happens from here is just icing on the cake."

Still, Patrick admits her NASCAR career is a work in progress. "I really wanted to come out of the box and kind of blow people away," she says. "There was some of that, and there was a lot of *not* that. … Sometimes it's moving faster than other times, sometimes it's moving a little bit slow for what I want. … But I think that it is going in the right direction, and that's all I can ask for."

Awards and Recognition

Despite the challenges she has faced in NASCAR, Patrick has received lots of awards and recognition—both in the cockpit and out.

In 2005, Patrick won both Indianapolis 500 Rookie of the Year and IndyCar Series Rookie of the Year. She was also voted IndyCar Series Most Popular Driver—an honor she held for six consecutive years, until 2010. (The next year, fans voted in Dan Wheldon, who had been killed at Las Vegas, as a tribute to his memory.) Her merchandise outsold that of all other drivers by a margin of ten to one. Patrick also was named NASCAR Nationwide Series Most Popular Driver in 2012, her first year as a full-time driver.

She has received other awards, too. In 2005, she was named Female Athlete of the Year by the United States Sports Academy and USAToday.com—beating out Maria Sharapova, the Williams sisters, and Michelle Wie. (That same year, she was nominated for an ESPY for Best Breakthrough athletic performance but lost to NBA star Dwyane Wade.) In 2006, the March of Dimes awarded Patrick the title of Sportswoman of the Year. In 2008, after she won the IndyCar race at Motegi, Japan, the governor of Patrick's home state, Illinois, honored Patrick with her own day: April 26, 2008. And between 2008 and 2011, Patrick won the Nickelodeon Kids' Choice award for favorite female athlete.

Causes Close to Patrick's Heart

As wonderful as it is to receive accolades and awards, Patrick knows it's better to give than to receive. She is a big believer in giving back. "I support a number of charitable causes," Patrick recently told a reporter. "Especially those geared toward children and animals."

Most recently, Patrick supported the No Kid Hungry campaign, which is dedicated to ending child hunger in the United States. She also supports Rescue Ranch, which, according to its web site, promotes "respect for all animals, as well as agricultural, environmental, and wildlife conservation, and facilitates rehabilitation, rescue, and responsible pet ownership in order to enhance the human-animal bond."

That's not all. She frequently gives her time to visit ill children in hospitals, and is involved with the Make-A-Wish Foundation, which grants the wishes of children who suffer from life-threatening illnesses. And, she has partnered with NASCAR to encourage kids to pursue careers in the fields of science, technology, engineering, and mathematics (STEM).

One personal cause is raising awareness of Chronic Obstructive Pulmonary Disease (COPD). This disease killed Patrick's grandmother Barb at the age of sixty-one. "In the end, she was in a wheelchair, on oxygen twenty-four hours a day," Patrick says. "Her quality of life was very compromised. It was sad to see." In 2010, she served as a celebrity spokesperson for the Drive4COPD campaign, in support of the COPD Foundation, which is dedicated to raising awareness of this disease and helping people get screened for it.

Danica Patrick Scorecard

Career Highlights: Won the World Karting Association Grand National Championship (1994, 1996, 1997); finished second at Formula Ford Festival (2000); signed with Rahal Letterman Racing (2002); competed for RLR in Toyota Atlantic series, finishing sixth (2003) and third (2004) overall; started and finished the Indianapolis 500 in fourth position, led a women's record nineteen laps (2005); signed with Andretti Green Racing in IndyCar (2007); finished a career-high fifth in IndyCar standings (2009); competed for JR Motorsports full-time in NASCAR Nationwide Series, finishing tenth overall (2012); signed with Stewart-Haas Racing (2013); won the pole, led four laps and finished eighth, the best-ever finish for a woman at the Daytona 500 (2013).

First Woman to: Win an IndyCar pole (2005, Kansas); finish on the podium at the Indy 500 (third in 2009); win an IndyCar Race (2008 at Motegi, Japan); finish as high as fourth in a Nationwide Series event (2011, Las Vegas); win a Sprint Cup pole (2013, Daytona); complete a full Sprint Cup schedule (2013); finish as high as sixth in a Sprint Cup Series event (2014, Atlanta).

Honors: Named IndyCar Series and Indy 500 Rookie of the Year (2005); named Female Athlete of the Year by the United States Sports Academy and USAToday.com (2005); named IndyCar's most popular driver (2005-2010); named Nationwide Series most popular driver (2012); named sportswoman of the year by the March of Dimes (2006); won the Nickelodeon Kids' Choice Award as favorite female athlete (2008-2011).

Danica Patrick has appeared in countless advertisements and served as a spokesperson for many causes, including the Got Milk campaign.

Patrick Mania in the Media

Even when she's out of the car, Patrick remains in the public eye. Since she burst onto the scene in 2005, she has appeared on countless TV shows and commercials. Naturally, these include various talk shows and morning programs. She has also appeared in some shows you might not expect. For example, in 2010, Patrick made her acting debut on an episode of *CSI: NY*, in which she portrayed a race car driver suspected of murder. She was also featured in an episode of *The Simpsons*. As for commercials, Patrick has appeared in thirteen Super Bowl ads (more than any other celebrity)—all for GoDaddy, which sponsored her from 2007 until 2016. She's also been featured in commercials for Secret deodorant, ESPN, Honda cars, and other products.

Courting Controversy

Perhaps Patrick's most famous magazine appearance was in a 2003 issue of *FHM* magazine, in which she posed semi-nude alongside a classic car. These pictures sparked some controversy. "I'm not, and have not been, happy with those provocative photos that will be floating around on the Web forever," racing pioneer Janet Guthrie told one reporter. "It's sort of been the gestalt forever and ever that women have nothing to sell but their bodies."

Patrick took a more pragmatic view. "It helped me get the ride," she says of the photos. "The bottom line is, it takes money to go racing. If there's money there, and it puts me in a really good car, then I can go show what I can do." She explains, "Getting my break as a driver had nothing to do with being an attractive female. For me, just being a woman isn't going to do it. I still have to perform." However, she concedes, being an attractive female "didn't hurt me either."

Patrick understands that not all female athletes feel as she does. "Some women in sports have remained reluctant to use their looks or their femininity to capitalize or exploit their roles." But the way she sees it, she might as well use whatever assets she has. "It's obvious I'm a girl," she says, "so why not use it as a tool?" Besides, she says, "You gotta rock what you've got."

Similarly, magazine publishers can't get enough of her. She's appeared on the cover of *Sports Illustrated* and in the pages of that magazine's swimsuit issue. She's also appeared on the cover of *ESPN: The Magazine* and *TV Guide*.

Patrick has even appeared in a video game—*Sonic & All-Stars Racing Transformed*—and in three music videos, for Miranda Lambert, Colt Ford, and Jay-Z.

Getting Personal: Divorce and a New Love

In November 2012, just one day after their seventh wedding anniversary, Patrick and her husband Paul Hospenthal made a sad announcement: They were splitting up. Patrick posted on Facebook:

> I am sad to inform my fans that after seven years, Paul and I have decided to amicably end our marriage. This isn't easy for either of us, but mutually it has come to this. He has been an important person and friend in my life and that's who we will remain moving forward.

Patrick has remained silent on what caused the split. In court documents, she reported only that "My marriage is irretrievably broken, and there is no reasonable prospect of reconciliation."

Two months later, in January 2013, Patrick revealed that she had a new love: fellow NASCAR driver Ricky Stenhouse Jr. Born in Memphis, Tennessee, and raised in Olive Branch, Mississippi, Ricky is five years younger than Patrick. As of the start of 2017, the two remain a couple but are not married.

Patrick and Ricky are "opposite in almost every way," she says. "The truth is there are more misunderstandings than understandings

Ricky Stenhouse Jr.

Ricky Stenhouse Jr. made his debut in NASCAR in 2009, running a limited schedule in the Nationwide Series. He competed in six races and posted one top-five finish. The next year, Stenhouse competed in the Nationwide Series full-time. He scored five top-tens, two top-fives, and one podium—a third place at Daytona. He finished sixteenth overall and won Rookie of the Year honors.

In 2011, Stenhouse really came alive on the track. He dominated the Nationwide Series, pulling two poles, ten top-tens, seven top fives, six podiums, and two wins (both at Iowa), and winning the championship.

Danica Patrick meets on the track with new love Ricky Stenhouse Jr.

(Stenhouse also ran in one Sprint Cup race, finishing in eleventh.) Incredibly, 2012 went even better for Stenhouse. That year, he earned four poles, seven top-tens, five top-fives, eight podiums, and six wins, once again landing on top in the points.

Clearly, Stenhouse had earned a full-time ride in Sprint Cup, and in 2013, he got one, with Roush Fenway Racing. However, he hasn't been as successful there as one might have expected. In the three years since, he's earned one pole, ten top-tens, four top-fives, and three podiums, but no victories.

The Importance of Role Models

Patrick takes her job as a role model seriously. "I have to factor in that I have a young fan base that looks up to me," she says. "It's a responsibility I am so flattered to have ... I'm so grateful for the opportunity to be a woman raising the bar for other girls—future champions coming up behind me, whether they are drivers, politicians, doctors, teachers, whatever they dream they can be." Back in 2006, Patrick noted, "One of the most rewarding aspects of all the attention I've received this past year is showing the world that women can do anything ... But it's not just about a woman competing in a male-dominated sport. It's about being the best at whatever you do, regardless of gender."

For these young women, says St. James, Patrick "has eliminated the question in the minds of many: Can a woman win at the top level? It's tough, but what Danica did helps a lot."

Bob Rahal, Patrick's first boss in IndyCar, shares this view. In 2006, he said:

> Being a woman in this extremely male-oriented sport has had a huge impact on the sport. There is no doubt that her presence in the IRL has brought a new fan base to the sport. Not just young girls who have their own aspirations of someday driving like Danica did but also older fans who love this young girl on the

Danica Patrick: Breaking Speed Barriers

track beating the boys. She has brought back fans that have left the sport, repairing the rift between CART and Indy and in the process, Danica has created new opportunities for fans and drivers alike to enjoy the rising popularity of Indy racing.

Simply put, Patrick has had an incredible effect on motorsports. But for her, it's about being the best driver—not the best girl driver. "I'd love for people to look back and remember me as a great driver. If they remember me as a girl second, that's the way I prefer it. I want people to say she was a great driver and she kicked butt."

About the Author

Kate Shoup has written more than forty books and has edited hundreds more. When not working, Kate loves to watch IndyCar racing, ski, read, and ride her motorcycle. She lives in Indianapolis with her husband, her daughter, and their dog. To learn more about Kate and her work, visit www.kateshoup.com.